OLYMPIC SPORTS

TRACK AND FIELD

by Clive Gifford

amicus

Published by Amicus
P.O. Box 1329
Mankato, MN 56002

Printed in the United States of America, at Corporate Graphics in North Mankato, Minnesota.

Library of Congress Cataloging-in-Publication Data
Gifford, Clive.
 Track and Field / Clive Gifford.
    p. cm. -- (Olympic sports)
 Includes index.
 ISBN 978-1-60753-187-6 (hardcover, library binding)
 1. Track and field--Juvenile literature. 2. Olympics--Juvenile literature. I. Title.
 GV1060.55.G536 2012
 796.42--dc22

                        2010035184

Created by Appleseed Editions, Ltd.
Designed by Helen James
Edited by Mary-Jane Wilkins
Picture research by Su Alexander

Picture credits
Page 4 Getty Images; 5 AFP/Getty Images; 6 Sports Illustrated/Getty Images; 7 AFP/ Getty Images; 8 & 9 Sports Illustrated/Getty Images; 10 Jonathan Larsen/ Shutterstock; 11 AFP/Getty Images; 12 AFP/Getty Images; 13 Pete Niesen/ Shutterstock; 14 & 15 Getty Images; 16 Sports Illustrated/Getty Images; 17 & 18 Getty Images; 19 & 20 AFP/Getty Images; 21 & 22 Getty Images; 23, 24 & 25 AFP/ Getty Images; 26 Getty Images; 27t Muzsy/Shutterstock, b AFP/Getty Images; 28t AFP/Getty Images, b Getty Images; 29t AFP/Getty Images, b Getty Images
Front cover: AFP Getty Images

DAD0051
3-2011

9 8 7 6 5 4 3 2 1

Contents

4   Going for Gold

6   Sprint Races

10 Relay Races

12 Hurdles

14 Longer Races

16 The Marathon

18 Long Jump

20 High Jump

22 Discus

24 Javelin

26 Other Field Events

28 Gold Medal Greats

30 Glossary

31 Books and Web Sites

32 Index

Going for Gold

The Olympics is the greatest sporting event on Earth. More than 10,000 athletes (Olympians) flock to one country every four years to compete in their sport during 17 action-packed days. Winning an Olympic gold, silver, or bronze medal for finishing first, second, or third in an event is the highlight of many athletes' sports careers.

The U.S. 4 x 400m relay team (from left to right: LaShawn Merritt, Angelo Taylor, David Neville, and Jeremy Wariner) with their gold medals at the 2008 Beijing Olympics.

ANCIENT ATHLETICS

The ancient Olympics began in Greece in 776 BC. At first, there was just one event, a race over a distance called a *stade* (about 623 ft. or 190 m), from which the word stadium comes. Over time, other events were added. Most were track and field events, such as races run over varying distances, or throwing and jumping events including the discus and long jump.

MODERN GAMES

The ancient Olympics were held for more than 1,000 years before they were banned by the Roman emperor Theodosius. He was a

Christian who believed that the games were **pagan**. Then in 1896, the Olympics were revived at the first modern Olympic games held in Athens, Greece. Athletes competed in swimming and other sports, but track and field was center stage and has remained so ever since. Track events include running and **racewalking**, and field events involve jumping, throwing, and vaulting competitions.

DECATHLON AND HEPTATHLON

Athletes compete on both track and field in two events. The seven-event **heptathlon** for women and the ten-event **decathlon** for men are both held over two days of intense competition. Each athlete's time in a race, or distance covered in a jump or throw, is converted into points, and the winner is the athlete with the most points.

British athlete Jessica Ennis competes in the long jump at the 2010 World Indoor Championships. As a leading heptathlete, Ennis is trying for a medal at the 2012 Olympics.

FEATS AND RECORDS

The first modern Olympic games event was a field event—the triple jump. The winner, American James Connolly, came in second in the high jump and third in the long jump.

Sprint Races

The fastest men and women on the planet compete in races over distances that range from 60 meter sprints held indoors to 400 meters, or a complete **lap** of the track. To become the Olympic champion in the 100 meter is one of sport's greatest prizes.

In 2008, Jamaican Usain Bolt (wearing number 7) drives out of the blocks at the start of the 100 meter Olympic final, where he shattered the world record with a time of 9.69 seconds.

QUICK OFF THE BLOCKS

Competition is fierce in sprinting, and athletes run a number of races called **heats**. Only the fastest eight reach the final. Athletes begin in a crouching position, with their feet on angled supports called **starting blocks**. When the starter pistol fires, they power off their blocks.

FALSE STARTS

Sprinters need a fast start, but if they move too soon, the electronic sensors on their starting blocks signal a false start. In the past, a sprinter with two false starts was **disqualified**. In 2010, the starting rules were changed. Now, the first athlete to make a false start is disqualified.

RACE PACE

As they leave their blocks, sprinters drive forward from a low position and gradually straighten up until they are upright and reach their top speed. This can be as fast as 25 mph (40 km/h). Sprinters concentrate on a smooth and flowing running style and try to maintain their top speed, or pace, right to the finish line. Athletes complete a race when their chest crosses the finish line, rather than their legs or head.

Olympic OoPs

British sprinter Linford Christie won silver at the 1988 Olympics and gold at the 1992 games, but in the 1996 100 meter final, she was disqualified after two false starts.

FEATS AND RECORDS

At 16, American Betty Robinson became the first women's track gold medalist when she won the 100 meter at the 1928 Olympics. These were the first games to include track and field events for women.

PHOTO FINISHES

Some races are amazingly close, and officials use high-speed cameras to look at photo finishes to decide on a runner's position. At the 2008 Olympics, Jamaican sprinters Sherone Simpson and Kerron Stewart both finished the 100 meter sprint with the same time of 10.98 seconds and could not be separated into second and third, so they were both awarded silver medals.

Jamaica's Shelly-Ann Fraser (third from right) wins gold in the women's 100 meter sprint at the 2008 Olympics. A total of 85 sprinters took part in the women's 100 meter competition.

Michael Johnson (left) streaks ahead of Roger Black (second left) during the 1996 400 meter final. Johnson set a new Olympic record for the race, finishing in 43.49 seconds. Roger Black won the silver medal.

THE 200 METER SPRINT

The 200 meter race begins on the bend of the track and ends when the runners cross the finish line at the end of the **home straight.** Instead of starting in a straight line across the track, 200 meter runners have a staggered start so that they all run the same distance. Runners must stay in their lane, and they usually lean a little into the bend. They reach maximum speed when they power out of the bend and run down the straight, but face a challenge to keep that speed up all the way to the finish line.

DOUBLING UP

Many sprinters enter both the 100 and 200 meter races at the Olympics. A handful of superb athletes have won both, including the exciting Jamaican runner, Usain Bolt, who also added the 4 x 100 meter relay (see page 10) to his 2008 Olympic successes.

THE 400 METER SPRINT

Athletes also have a staggered start in this race. The distance between each athlete's starting position is greater because runners race around two complete bends in the track. Top Olympians today run this race as an all-out sprint, running

Superstar

Wilma Rudolph suffered from scarlet fever, whooping cough, and polio as a child, which left her left leg twisted and in a brace. Rudolph worked incredibly hard to recover, and at the 1960 Olympics won gold medals in the 100 and 200 meter, as well as the relay.

FEATS AND RECORDS

At the 1904 Olympics, the 200 meter race had no bend, as it was held on a straight course. U.S. athlete Archie Hahn won in a record time of 21.6 seconds. His Olympic record was not broken until 1932.

A DIFFICULT DOUBLE

Not many athletes have won both the 200 and 400 meter races. In 1996, something amazing happened. Both Michael Johnson and Marie-José Pérec of France won their 200 and 400 meter events. Both also set new Olympic record times, which have not yet been beaten.

each 100 meters in a little more than 11 seconds. American Michael Johnson's 400m world record stands at just 43.18 seconds.

Jamaican star sprinter Veronica Campbell-Brown crosses the line ahead of her rivals to win the Olympic 200 meter in 2008 in 21.74 seconds, the fastest time recorded in ten years.

Relay Races

Relay races are team events for four runners. Each runner covers the same distance, running one at a time while carrying a hollow metal tube called a **baton**. The baton is then passed to the next runner in the relay—this is called an exchange or change over.

Runners exchange the baton in the men's 4 x 400m relay at the 2004 Olympics. Teams try to lose as little time as possible during the exchange.

FAST AND FURIOUS

Men ran the 4 x 100 meter relay for the first time at the 1912 Olympics. The first women's race was run in 1928. It is one of the most exciting track races. The four team members each run such a fast lap of the track that the men's world record of 37.10 seconds is more than six seconds faster than the individual 400m world record.

FEATS AND RECORDS
One of the oldest Olympic records still standing was set by the East German women's 100 meter relay team, who won gold in 41.60 seconds in 1980.

CHANGING OVER

The lightning speed of the runners in the 4 x 100 meter relay means that every runner must time their start and baton exchange accurately. The exchange takes place on a 20 meter section of the track called the **changeover** zone. If runners do not exchange the baton within the zone, or a runner strays out of the lane, their team is disqualified.

THE 4 X 400 METER RELAY

The first runner in a 4 x 400 meter race runs a lap in one lane. The runner passes the baton to the second runner, who runs past a line called the **break line** after 100 meters. At this point, all the runners leave their lanes and head to the inside lane, which is the shortest distance around the track. The third **leg** runner and the **anchor** (the final runner) both run on the inside lane.

DROPPED!

A runner who drops the baton in either the 4 x 100 or 4 x 400 races is not disqualified, but recovering the baton loses vital seconds, so the team continues the race a long way behind its competitors.

Runners in the Russian 4 x 100 relay team exchange the baton during the 2008 Olympic final. The Russians won, with Belgium second, and Nigeria third.

Hurdles

DOHA 2010

Cuba's Dayron Robles won the 2008 Olympics 110 meter hurdles in 12.93 seconds. He was the only hurdler under 13 seconds in the final.

Hurdles are barriers placed in set positions across the track that athletes jump over as they race around the track. There are three different hurdling events at the Olympics.

SPRINT HURDLES

Women run sprint hurdle races over 100 meters, and men race over 110 meters. Athletes clear ten hurdles between the start and finish line, using a technique they perfect over years of training. The hurdles fall easily if they are touched. This allows runners to continue racing, but sometimes a runner falls as a result.

THE 400 METER HURDLES

Men first ran the 400 meter hurdles race at the 1900 Olympics, but women had to wait until 1984 to compete. During the race, athletes clear ten barriers around the track. Each runner stays in one lane, just as in a regular 400 meter race. They need to hit the right **stride pattern** between hurdles, which is hard near the end of a race when their leg muscles tire.

Top hurdlers complete the race in only three or four more seconds than runners in races without hurdles. The U.S. men's hurdlers have a terrific record at the Olympics, and have won 18 of the 24 competitions. In 2008, they took home all three medals.

The 100m hurdles is often an incredibly close race. The 2008 women's 100m Olympic final was won by U.S. hurdler Dawn Harper.

THE STEEPLECHASE

This exciting event is run over 3,000 meters. Men have competed in the steeplechase since 1896, but the first women's event was held at the 2008 Olympics. Competitors jump 28 large hurdles across the track and clear a water jump seven times during the race. Despite the obstacles, steeplechasers run at high speeds throughout the race. The 2008 women's gold medalist, Russia's Gulnara Galkina-Samitova, broke the world record with a scorching time of 8 minutes, 58.81 seconds.

Olympic OoPs

Finland's Volmari Iso-Hollo won the 1932 Olympic steeplechase in a time of 10:33.4, a minute slower than the time he ran to qualify. This was because an official forgot how many laps had been run and all competitors ran an extra lap.

Superstar

U.S. athlete Edwin Moses is the greatest 400 meter hurdler of all time. Between 1977 and 1987, he ran in 122 races and won them all! This included two Olympic races in which he won gold medals, in 1976 and 1984.

Steeplechasers clear the water jump in the men's 2008 Olympic final. The race was won by Kenya's Brimin Kipruto, who became the seventh Kenyan in a row to win this event.

Longer Races

When athletes run longer races, they need huge powers of **endurance**. Their goal is to survive the fast and grueling pace, and to keep enough energy in reserve to sprint for the line at the finish.

Britain's Kelly Holmes raises her arms as she wins her second gold medal of the 2004 games, the 1,500 meter, with Russia's Tatyana Tomashova coming second, and Maria Cioncan of Romania third.

MIDDLE DISTANCE RACING

The 800 and 1,500 meter are the middle distance events at an Olympics. Runners complete each lap at high speed and try to save a little energy for a sprint to the finish line. A number of athletes double up and enter both races, but only five (two men and three women) have won both at the same Olympics. The last athlete to do this was Kelly Holmes of Britain.

THE 5,000 METER

This race is a test of speed and **stamina**, as runners increase speed in the last laps. At the Olympics, 15 runners compete in the 5,000 meter final, selected from the fastest runners in three heats. The first four finishers in each heat plus the three fastest losers overall enter the final. Until 1996, women ran only 3,000 meters.

THE 10,000 METER

This is the longest track race at the Olympics. Men first ran it in 1912 and women in 1988. Athletes run 25 laps at a fast, even pace. They keep an eye on their rivals, who try to break away into a lead, while saving enough energy to make a dash for the finish line in the last laps. Athletes run each lap of the track in not much more than a minute.

AMAZING AFRICANS

African runners have won almost all the medals in the men's 5,000 and 10,000 meter at recent Olympics. Only one of the 18 medals awarded for the 10,000 meter in the past six Olympics has gone to a non-African runner. Ethiopia's Kenenisa Bekele holds the record of 27 minutes, 5.1 seconds. Tirunesh Dibaba, also from Ethiopia, holds the women's record of 29 minutes, 54.66 seconds. In 2008, she won both the 5,000 and 10,000 meter Olympic races.

Ethiopia's Tariku Bekele leads the pack as they run down the track straight during the 5,000m final of the 2008 games. Bekele finished sixth, and his brother, Kenenisa, won the gold medal.

The Marathon

The longest running race at the Olympics is the marathon. It is named after the legend of Pheidippides, an ancient Greek messenger who is said to have run from the Battle of Marathon to Athens around 490 BC.

Kenyan marathon runner Samuel Kamau Wanjiru crosses the line to win the gold medal at the 2008 games. His time was nearly three minutes faster than the previous record.

OLYMPIC COURSES

Since the 1924 games, the marathon course has been 26.22 miles (42.195 km) long. Each course varies depending on the **terrain** of the city where the games are held. At the 2012 games, the course runs through central London past many famous landmarks before reaching the Olympic stadium. At the end of every Olympic marathon, runners enter the athletics stadium and complete one lap of the track to finish.

Superstar

Abebe Bikila won the 1960 Olympic marathon in bare feet. The Ethiopian athlete competed at the last minute and had no running shoes that fit him. Bikila won the marathon again in 1964—this time wearing shoes.

Along the Way

Running a marathon is a grueling task. In the men's 2008 marathon, 22 of the 98 competitors who started did not finish the race. There are refreshment tables alongside the course at 3.1 mile (5 km) intervals where runners can grab a sports drink or water while running. Sponging stations also line the route, allowing runners to squeeze a sponge soaked in cold water over their heads and bodies.

Pace and Stamina

It's sometimes hard to judge from television images just how fast athletes are running in a marathon. Top marathon runners cover every mile in about five minutes (three minutes per km) and keep up this pace over the entire race. The 2008 men's winner, Samuel Kamau Wanjiru, set a new Olympic record of 2 hours, 6 minutes,

32 seconds. Constantina Dita of Romania won the women's race in 2 hours, 26 minutes, 44 seconds, and at the age of 38 became the oldest Olympic marathon winner in history.

Olympic OoPs

Early Olympic marathons weren't always carefully checked. American Fred Lorz crossed the line first at the 1904 marathon and was greeted by cheering crowds, only to admit later that he had taken a ride in a car for 10.6 miles (17 km) of the race.

Top runners cross Tower Bridge during the 2010 London Marathon. The race was won for the first time by Russian athlete Liliya Shobukhova.

Long Jump

The long jump is one of the most explosive of all field events. Competitors sprint fast down a narrow strip of track called the **runway** and leap as far as they can, landing in a long sandpit.

RUN-UPS AND NO JUMPS

Long jumpers pace their run-up very carefully. Their goal is to reach maximum speed before they leap off a panel in front of the sandpit called the take-off board. They must place the foot on or behind the board. If they overstep the board, officials wave a red flag to signal a **no jump** that doesn't count, even if it is very long.

GOOD LANDING

Jumpers try to stay in the air as long as they can. When they land, they collapse their legs into the sand and try to avoid leaning back or placing their hands behind them. This is because each jump is measured from the take-off board to the nearest mark that the athlete's body has made in the sand.

Jade Johnson flies through the air during the 2008 Olympic long jump. Johnson's longest jump of 6.64 meters (21.78 ft.) was 40 cm (15.75 in.) shorter than the winning jump of Maurren Higa Maggi.

CHAMPION JUMPERS

The men's long jump has been part of every modern Olympics. U.S. jumpers have won 21 of the 26 competitions held. Women first competed in the long jump at the 1948 Olympics and winners have come from all over the world, including New Zealander Yvette Williams, German Heike Drecshler, and Brazilian Maurren Higa Maggi, who became the 2008 champion.

SPRINTING SUCCESS

Top long jumpers need speed on the runway, and some leading jumpers are also successful sprint racers. U.S. Olympic legend Jesse Owens won four gold medals in the long jump and sprint races at the 1936 games. The year before, Owens had jumped 8.13 m (26.67 ft.), a world record that lasted 25 years!

Superstar

The most successful of all Olympic long jumpers is American Carl Lewis, who won four Olympic long jump gold medals, as well as five other Olympic gold medals in sprint races.

FEATS AND RECORDS

Irving Saladino became Panama's first ever Olympic champion in any sport in 2008 when he won the long jump competition with a leap of 8.34 meters (27.36 ft.). He returned home to a parade of thousands of people.

Panama's Irving Saladino lands after his gold medal-winning long jump of 8.34 meters (27.36 ft.) at the 2008 Olympics. It was his country's first Olympic gold.

High Jump

The high jump is one of the most exciting field events. Athletes need rhythm, **flexibility**, and explosive jumping power as they leap over a bar often set at a height far above their heads.

Bryan Clay takes off vertically at the start of a high jump attempt in the men's decathlon. High jumpers try for a powerful spring up and over the bar.

JUMP STYLE

The high jump is a 13 foot (4 m) long bar that rests on supports. Jumpers are allowed to touch the bar as they jump, but it must stay on the supports for the jump to count. In the past, jumpers used all sorts of techniques. Then in 1968 American Dick Fosbury stunned rivals

FEATS AND RECORDS
Javier Sotomayor from Cuba set the men's world record in 1993, a year after he won Olympic gold. His leap of 2.45 meters (8.04 ft.) has never been beaten.

with a head-first technique called the Fosbury flop. This is used by all top athletes today.

THREE ATTEMPTS
Olympic high jumpers usually have three attempts at each height. If they fail to clear the bar after the third attempt, they are out of the competition. As jumpers succeed at a height, the bar is raised and every jumper has three attempts at clearing the new height. The competition continues until only one athlete clears a height.

COUNTBACK
The distances separating high jumpers are often tiny. If more than one athlete clears the winning

Superstar
Iolanda Balas of Romania not only won two Olympic gold medals in the women's high jump, she also broke the world record 14 times. Between 1957 and 1967, she won 140 high jump competitions in a row!

height, the winner is the one who made the fewest attempts. This is known as **countback**. At the 2008 games, Blanka Vlasic and Tia Hellebaut both cleared 2.05 meters (6.73 ft.), but Hellebaut won gold and Vlasic silver since Vlasic needed more attempts to clear that height.

Tia Hellebaut of Belgium clears the bar during the Olympic women's high jump competition, which she won. Her winning jump of 2.05 meters (6.73 ft.) was her best ever.

Discus

Athletes throw the discus using a sweeping arm movement. The first event was held at the ancient Olympics in 708 BC using a stone and bronze discus. The men's discus competition has been part of every modern Olympics, and the women's competition was first held in 1928.

American Stephanie Brown Trafton wins the 2008 Olympic women's discus competition. Her victory was a surprise, as throwers from Russia, Germany, and Eastern Europe have dominated women's discus at the Olympics.

FEATS AND RECORDS

French athlete Micheline Ostermeyer won the gold medal in the 1948 women's discus event. She also won gold in the shot put and a bronze in the high jump.

THROWING CIRCLE

A discus thrower starts at the back of an 8 foot wide (2.5 m) throwing circle. Throwers enter the circle from the back and use every bit of the circle space as they turn around and around, making long rhythmic swings led by the arm holding the discus.

AROUND AND AROUND

Throwers spin around, building speed and power, until their bodies face the front of the circle. The arm and hand holding the discus is behind and whips forward past the rest of the body with enormous power. Then, the thrower releases the discus, pressing the fingers on its edge to help it spin away smoothly.

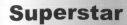

Gerd Kanter releases the discus from the throwing circle that has a safety cage around it to protect spectators. The 12 throwers in a discus final have three throws each.

LONG DISTANCE DISCUS

The discus is one event in which women have thrown longer distances than men. This is partly because a woman's discus weighs 2.2 lbs (1 kg) and a men's discus 4.4 lbs (2 kg). With a well-timed, powerful throw, top Olympic athletes can throw the discus well over 60 meters (197 ft.).

WORLD RECORD THROWS

In the men's discus, no one has beaten Jürgen Schult's world record of 74.08 meters (243.04 ft.). The German set this world record years ago, in 1986. During the 1970s, Ukrainian Faina Melnik broke the women's world record 11 times and won the gold medal at the 1972 Olympics.

Javelin

Javelin throwers need skill and timing, as well as strength, to hurl the javelin over long distances. Top throwers can send the javelin away at speeds of more than 62 mph (100 km/h).

Norway's Andreas Thorkildsen draws back the javelin just before unleashing it during the men's javelin final at the Beijing games in 2008. Thorkildsen repeated his 2004 gold medal success in Beijing.

THE JAVELIN

In the ancient Olympics, the javelin was a straight branch cut from an olive tree. Until the 1950s, many competitors used a bamboo javelin. Today, the javelin is a hollow metal tube around 8.5 ft. (2.6 m) long for men, and 7.2 ft. (2.2 m) long for women. It has a sharp point and a cord grip around halfway down its length.

RUNWAY AND TAKE-OFF

Javelin throwers start each throw at the end of a narrow corridor called a runway. They build up speed holding the javelin level with the ground at head height. Turning to face the side, they draw the javelin back, then whip their arm and body forward to unleash it with explosive power. The distances thrown can be enormous. At the 2008

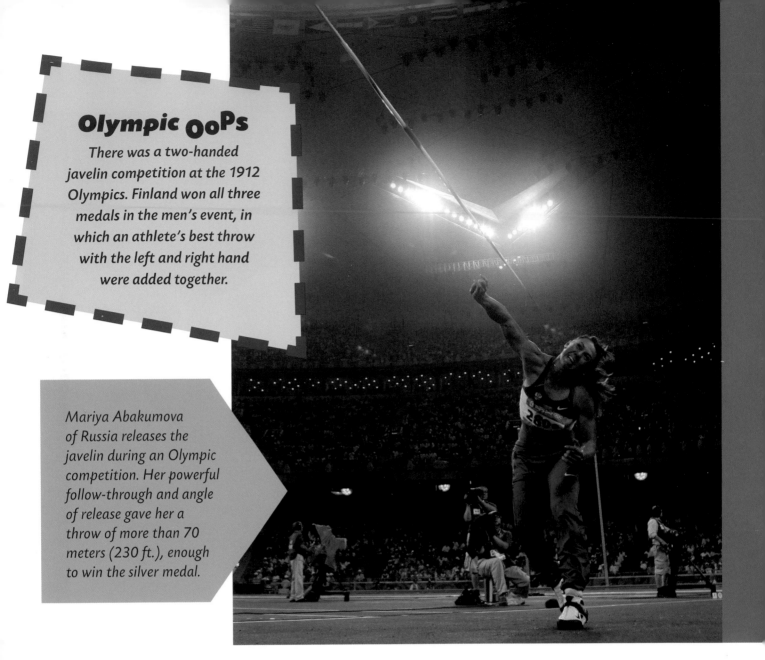

Mariya Abakumova of Russia releases the javelin during an Olympic competition. Her powerful follow-through and angle of release gave her a throw of more than 70 meters (230 ft.), enough to win the silver medal.

games, Norway's Andreas Thorkildsen won gold with a throw of 90.57 meters (297.15 ft.), the longest ever at an Olympics.

A WINNING THROW

A winning throw has to be long, but also straight so that it lands in the throwing sector. Throwers try to release the javelin at an angle so that it lands nose first, otherwise officials signal a **no throw**. In the Olympics final, competitors are allowed three throws and the top eight athletes then have three more throws each.

Superstar

Jan Zelezny of the Czech Republic won silver in the 1988 Olympics and went on to greater success in the 1990s. He won gold medals at the 1992, 1996, and 2000 Olympics. His 1996 world record throw was an amazing 98.48 meters (323.10 ft.).

Other Field Events

A number of other field athletics events are held at the Olympics and at other major international athletics competitions.

U.S. shot-putter Reese Hoffa cradles the shot beside his neck before leaning back and then driving forward explosively to put the shot. Shot-putters dust their hands with chalk for a good grip.

SHOT PUT

The shot is a solid metal ball weighing 16 lbs (7.26 kg) for men and 8.8 lbs (4 kg) for women. Shot-putters cradle the ball in one hand while standing in a small throwing circle, then swivel around, throwing the arm up and out to launch the shot into the air. The 2008 Olympic champions—Tomasz Majewski of Poland and Valerie Vili of New Zealand—regularly throw the shot more than 20 meters (66 ft.).

Olympic OoPs

While practicing shortly before the shot put final, Randy Barnes was hit in the back by a shot from U.S. teammate John Godina. The accident didn't stop Barnes from winning gold with a throw of 21.62 meters (70.93 ft.). Godina won silver.

A hammer thrower builds speed and momentum in the circle by turning and swinging the hammer.

far as possible. Triple jumpers build speed before their jump with a hop leaping off one foot, then landing on it. They then take a long step, landing on the opposite foot, before jumping into the pit like a long jumper. The distances covered are amazing—Kenny Harrison set the Olympic record in 1996 with a jump of 18.09 meters (59.35 ft.).

THE HAMMER

The hammer is a shot put on a chain around 3 feet (1 m) long attached to a handle. The thrower swings the hammer around, building up speed and power, before stepping across the circle and releasing it. The hammer can soar long distances. Aksana Miankova of Belarus won the 2008 women's hammer with a throw of 76.34 meters (250.46 ft.).

POLE VAULT

Pole vaulters sprint down a runway and plant their pole in a small slot to vault up. The pole bends and then unbends, carrying the vaulter up around 5 meters (16 ft.) for women and 6 meters (20 ft.) for men. The goal is to clear a bar without knocking it off the supports.

TRIPLE JUMP

Triple jumps are performed on the same runway and pit as the long jump. Athletes try to jump as

FEATS AND RECORDS

The 1896 Olympic pole vault event was won by Welles Hoyt with a jump of 3.30 meters (10.83 ft.). At the 1988 Olympics, Sergey Bubka set an Olympic record of 5.90 meters (19.36 ft.) —five feet higher than a semi-truck!

Steven Hooker clears the bar after releasing his pole. The Australian athlete won the 2008 Olympic gold with a vault of 5.96 meters (19.55 ft.).

Gold Medal Greats

Many competitors train hard and make sacrifices to perform at their best in the Olympics. Competition is fierce in all sports, so only the most talented make it. Here are the stories of four great Olympic athletes.

USAIN BOLT

Nicknamed "Lightning" for good reasons, the Jamaican runner was disappointed when he didn't progress past the heat of his first Olympics in 2004. Bolt bounced back in sensational style at the 2008 Olympics, where he won the 100 meter, 200 meter, and 4 x 100 relay, all in astonishing world record times. His run of 9.69 seconds in the 100 meter could have been even faster, but he slowed down in the last 30 meters. Bolt beat both his 100 and 200 meter world records at the 2009 World Championships.

Usain Bolt performs his "lightning bolt" gesture in 2008.

FANNY BLANKERS-KOEN

The 1940 and 1944 Olympics were canceled because of World War II. So Dutchwoman Fanny Blankers-Koen first competed at the 1948 games. Women could only enter three individual events at these Olympics. She entered the 100 meter, 80 meter hurdles, and 200 meter and won them all. She won her fourth gold of the games in the 4 x 100 relay and might have won a fifth and sixth gold medal if she had been allowed to enter the long jump and high jump. Blankers-Koen was the outstanding performer at the 1948 Olympics, and was named female athlete of the century in 1999 by the IAAF, the organization that runs world athletics.

YELENA ISINBAYEVA

Isinbayeva was a Russian gymnast until 1998. Since then, she has become a star performer in the women's pole vault. In 2003, she broke the world record by clearing 4.84 meters (15.88 ft.). She won Olympic gold in 2004 and repeatedly broke the world record. At the 2008 Olympics, she set an amazing new high of 5.05 meters (16.57 ft.) to win her second gold medal.

PAAVO NURMI

Paavo Nurmi is Finland's long distance running star. He won a staggering nine Olympic gold medals in a range of races from 1,500 to 10,000 meters at three Olympics (1920, 1924, and 1928). He won five of the medals in just six days during the 1924 games—an astonishing feat. Nurmi also won three silver medals, including one in the 3,000 meter steeplechase in 1928, an event he had run only three times before.

The great Paavo Nurmi crosses the line to win a race in London.

29

Index

anchor 11

baton 10, 11
Blankers-Koen, Fanny 28, 29
Bolt, Usain 6, 8, 28
break line 11

changeover zone 11
countback 21

decathlon 5, 20
discus 4, 22–23
disqualification 6, 7, 11, 18, 25

endurance 14
exchange 10, 11

false starts 6, 7
flexibility 20

hammer 27
heptathlon 5
high jump 5, 20–21, 22
hurdles 12–13, 28

Isinbayeva, Yelena 29

javelin 24–25

long jump 4, 5, 18–19, 27

marathon 16–17

Nurmi, Paavo 29

pole vault 27, 29

racewalking 5
relay races 10–11
runway 18, 24, 27

shot-put 22, 26, 27, 29
sprint races 6–9, 19
stamina 14, 17
starting blocks 6, 7
steeplechase 13, 29
stride pattern 12
swimming 5

take-off board 18
terrain 16
throwing circle 22, 23, 26, 27
training 5, 12, 28
triple jump 5, 27